Memories of Vietnam

War in the First Person

Ellen Weiss

SCHOLASTIC INC.

New York   Toronto   London   Auckland   Sydney
Mexico City   New Delhi   Hong Kong   Buenos Aires

**Cover Illustration by
Alex Williamson**

Cover Photos

L: © Hulton-Deutsch Collection/Corbis,
R: © Jim Pickerell/Black Star.

Acknowledgments appear on page 64, which constitutes an extension of this copyright page.

ISBN 0-439-59807-9

15 14 13 12 11   23   12 11

Contents

Welcome to This Book

Have you ever wondered how you would act in a war? Would you be scared? Brave? Both?

During the 1960s, American soldiers headed halfway around the world to Vietnam. They went by the hundreds of thousands. And the lives of 58,160 Americans were lost before the U.S. troops were called back home in 1973.

Why did they go? What was it like? The people who were there will tell you. Read the letters of the soldiers, nurses, and volunteers. This is their story, told in their own words.

Target Words

These words will help you understand why United States soldiers were fighting in Vietnam.

- **conflict:** a war or period of fighting

  The conflict began when North Vietnam attacked South Vietnam.

- **escalate:** to increase in amount or intensity

  The number of U.S. troops in Vietnam escalated to over half a million.

- **influence:** to have an effect on something

  The United States wanted to influence the outcome of the war in Vietnam.

Reader Tips

Here's how to get the most out of this book.

- **Chapter Titles** A chapter title often expresses the chapter's main idea. Consider the chapter title as you read each letter. It will help you understand what that letter is about.

- **Fact/Opinion** As you read, think about what is a fact and what is an opinion. A fact is a statement that can be proven. An opinion is a statement about a personal feeling or belief. The letters contain plenty of both.

Time Line of the Vietnam War

Here is a brief history of the conflict from its roots to its final conclusion.

1800s: France controls the area known as Indochina, including Vietnam.

1954: The Communists in Vietnam declare war on the French and win. A peace treaty divides Vietnam in two. The North is Communist.

1956: South Vietnam cancels an election that the Communists in the South probably would have won.

1961: North Vietnam invades South Vietnam. The U.S. sends 3,000 soldiers to help the South.

1964: The U.S. begins bombing North Vietnam after they attack two war ships. The U.S. decides to send as many troops as needed to support South Vietnam.

1968: The U.S. now has more than 536,000 troops in Vietnam. The U.S. wins a bloody battle called the Tet Offensive. (Tet is the Vietnamese New Year.) But the battle claims the lives of 2,500 U.S. soldiers. The war is becoming unpopular back in the U.S.

1969: The U.S. president slowly begins to bring U.S. troops home.

1973: North and South Vietnam agree to stop fighting. Almost all U.S. troops are sent home.

1975: North Vietnam breaks the agreement. Its troops take over South Vietnam. Vietnam is reunited under Communist control and becomes one country again.

Map of Vietnam (1954–1975)

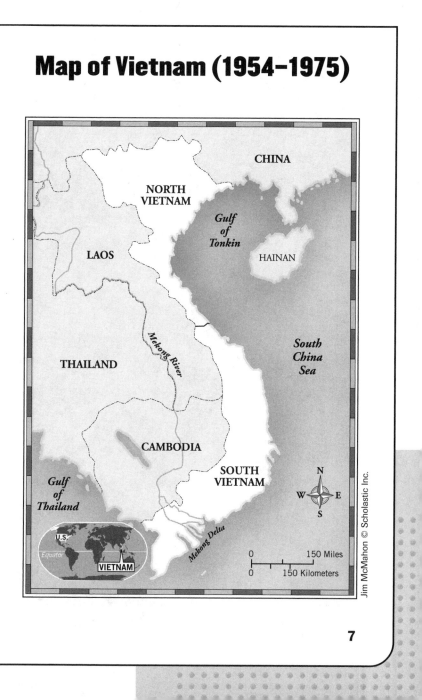

CHINA

NORTH VIETNAM

Gulf of Tonkin

HAINAN

LAOS

Mekong River

THAILAND

South China Sea

CAMBODIA

SOUTH VIETNAM

Gulf of Thailand

N
W   E
S

U.S.

Equator

VIETNAM

Mekong Delta

| 0 | | 150 Miles |
| 0 | | 150 Kilometers |

Jim McMahon © Scholastic Inc.

7

Soldiers wrote letters and shared their experiences in Vietnam with family and loved ones back home.

1

First Look at Vietnam

*Richard Ford, a **veteran,** looks back on his first day in Vietnam. It was nothing like he expected.*

When I stepped off the plane in Tan Son Nhut, that heat from the ground hit me in the face. And the odor from the climate was so strong. I said, "Where am I? What is this?" While we were walking off the plane, guys were coming toward the plane. And they said, "Happy Birthday, Merry Christmas, Happy Easter, I'll write your mom." They kept going. In other words, you will have Easter here, have a birthday here, and have Christmas here. And good luck.

—Richard Ford is retired. He used to track down drug smugglers for the U.S. government.

Rifleman Thomas Bird remembers his first experience in Vietnam. The reality of war came as a shock.

We got to the airstrip at Pleiku. Someone said to me, "Oh, man, go over to the [other side of the] airstrip. Get yourself a couple of extra pairs of boots." I was the only one who went across the airstrip. I started noting men's names in the boots, and I said, "These are somebody's boots. I don't want these boots." Then I noticed piles of uniforms with lots of blood. It hit me like a ton of bricks. All of a sudden I realized what was going on and where those guys were coming from. They were coming from [a battle at] Ia Drang [where I was going].

**—Thomas Bird works
in theater in New York City.**

─Heads Up!─

Thomas Bird looks at those extra boots and uniforms and realizes something about them. What does he realize?

Just after arriving in Vietnam, Paul O'Connell remembers watching members of Mike Company coming back from a month-long battle. This was the unit he would be joining.

The Marines looked nothing like any Marines I had ever seen. The spit and polish was long gone. Every one of them was weighted down with enormous packs on their backs. They could hardly lift their feet when they walked, and most of them needed a shave. Their trousers were rolled up to just below their knees. The bare skin on their legs was caked with a red-tinted mud.

**—Paul O'Connell is now a
deputy fire chief in Massachusetts.**

Heads Up!

Think about the expression "spit and polish." How does that help you picture what the Marines looked like before battle?

Us Against Them

After the end of World War II, two countries became superpowers in the world. One was the United States. The other was the Soviet Union.

These two powerful countries tried to **influence** as many other countries as they could. The Soviet Union supported countries that wanted **Communism.** The U.S. supported any government that was against Communism.

North Vietnam was a Communist state, but **South Vietnam** wasn't. When the **conflict** began, U.S. sent soldiers to defend South Vietnam.

U.S. soldiers had a tough fight. They were under attack from two armies. One army came from the North. Another was a rebel army from the South called the **Viet Cong**.

The Viet Cong were Communists, too. And they didn't want help from the U.S. They were on the side of the North. So, they fought the U.S. troops with **guerrilla warfare** and surprise attacks. They did not wear uniforms. They stayed hidden. It was hard for U.S. troops to fight them.

A Soldier's Life

Sergeant Salvador Gonzalez wrote this letter to his sister Connie, soon after arriving in Vietnam. He has one message for her and another for his mother!

January 14, 1969

This is to let you know that I'm OK. I want to tell you about that 12-day mission so that you can keep Mom from worrying. Don't show her this letter because the following is what I'll be doing for the next 11 months.

First it rained for six days solid. I got muddy and wet. My hands are covered with cuts. The jungles have thousands of **leeches** and mosquitoes. I think I have gotten bitten almost all over my body. I personally had to dig up two dead bodies. The smell was terrible. I just about got sick. About three or four guys got hurt through accidents.

The fighting is not heavy yet. But the rumor is we're moving south. I walk up and down mountains with a heavy pack on my back. But if everyone else does it, so can I. It's not so hard, actually. But one thing is for certain: you surely learn to appreciate some of the finer things you once had. Don't get me wrong. I'm not complaining or expecting sympathy. All I want to do is lay the line on what I'm doing. In return you must tell Mom that I'm probably out in the field doing hardly anything at all.

Love,
Sal

—Salvador Gonzalez is an electrical engineer. He lives in New York City.

Sergeant Henry Romero wrote this letter to his mother from the army base where he worked. In it, he talks about how powerful it was to celebrate Thanksgiving in Vietnam. It made him realize what he was doing there and what he was fighting for back at home.

November 27, 1969

I wrote you a letter this morning, but I just had to write you again and tell you about our Thanksgiving Day dinner. Well, all week I had this funny idea that because I had to be here in Vietnam I had nothing to be thankful for. But then I went to the mess hall to eat. I was really surprised. It was beautiful. They had Thanksgiving decorations all over. There was a white tablecloth on all the tables, Thanksgiving napkins and menus. We walked in and sat down and the dinner was brought to us. Then I realized that it was a symbol of what all of us soldiers had back home. I realized how wrong I was to feel that I had nothing to be thankful for.

When soldiers weren't fighting battles, they tried to make their lives in camp as normal as possible.

I can't tell you how proud I feel. Of course, I'm sad because I'm away from home. But I know that when my children grow up, the world they live in will be better than the world we live in now. I will feel content knowing that I helped.

Forever,

Henry

—Henry Romero survived the Vietnam War. He died in 1981 in a construction accident.

—Heads Up!—

Henry says his children will live in a better world. What makes that statement an opinion?

Snapshots of Vietnam

Vietnam was the first foreign land many U.S. soldiers had seen. Marine Mike Bailey shared these memories on a Web site set up by Vietnam veterans.

When we left Hill 10, our **platoon** split up. Each squad was sent to a different village. We were sent to work with the people. My platoon was going to a village called An Tan.

Our presence did not stop the day-to-day activity of this village. Two huts to the east there was an old gentleman of about 70 years. He would sit in his front yard in the early evening. He played tunes on a three-stringed instrument called a *samisen*. One day I brought my guitar over to him, thinking he would be interested in it. He smiled and kept playing.

Rice is the major crop in Vietnam. It is the single most important part of their daily diet, as in other countries in Asia. Many of the rice paddies were at different water levels. The water had to be moved around to each paddy, to make them all about 2–4 inches deep. This was so the rice could grow properly. Two women with a basket would move the water around. They would scoop the water out of the lower paddy. Then they dumped it into the paddy that needed the water. This hard job would be done from morning till evening, for days.

—Mike Bailey, a former Marine, served in Vietnam from 1968 to 1970.

Heads Up!

How do you think Mike feels about the village he describes? Why do you think so?

*During the war, American soldiers had a hard time telling the Viet Cong from the **civilians**. American soldiers often didn't know who the enemy was. In some cases, they burned whole villages down. Women and children were killed. Some of the soldiers found it hard to forgive themselves for these actions. Private George Williams wrote to his mother two months after he arrived in Vietnam.*

April 1967

How are things back in the World? I hope all is well! Things are pretty much the same. Vietnam has my feelings on a seesaw.

This country is so beautiful when the sun is shining on the mountains. I see farmers in their rice paddies, with their water buffalo. I love the palm trees, monkeys, birds and even the strange insects. For a moment I wasn't in a war zone at all, just on vacation.

There are a few kids who hang around, some with no parents. I feel so sorry for them. I do things to make them laugh. And they call me dinky dow. That means "crazy." But it makes me feel good. I hope that's one reason why we're

The American soldiers got to know the Vietnamese people who
lived nearby their army camps.

here, to win a future for them. It seems to be the only excuse I can think of for the things that I have done!

Love to all. Your son, George

—George Williams is a firefighter in Brooklyn, New York.

—Heads Up!—

Reread the last line of George's letter. How do you think George feels about the things he has done?

Suffering and Loss

Sergeant Kenneth Peeples, Jr. wrote his parents about a battle he was in. It took place just a month after he arrived in Vietnam.

July 3, 1966

I don't know how I can say this without alarming you. But I know I'll have to tell you about it. NBC News was there. I'm afraid you might have seen me on film or read about the dreadful fighting.

When I think about the hell I've been through the last few days, I can't help but cry. I wonder how I am still alive. My company suffered the worst losses. I believe it was something close to 50 dead and wounded. Friends I took training with have been killed. Some are seriously wounded. In my squad of nine men, only four of us survived.

This was the worst battle that this company has experienced.

How I made it, I don't know. Perhaps you didn't read about it, but in case you did I just wanted to tell you I'm OK.

I can't help crying now because I think about the horror of those three days. I was carrying the bodies of wounded and dead onto helicopters when I saw NBC. They were taking pictures.

Yesterday we were rescued from that area by helicopter. I thought they'd never come for us. The area is less than two miles from Cambodia, where VCs [Viet Cong soldiers] have regiments. They ambushed us.

Try to hold up. By the time you receive this, I hope to be somewhat recovered and at ease.

Love, Kenny

—Kenneth Peeples, Jr. was wounded in February, 1967. A librarian, he now lives in New Jersey.

Soldiers carried their wounded off the battlefield. Helicopters
would airlift some to hospitals in Tokyo, Japan.

John McCain was a U.S. Navy pilot. In 1967, he was shot down over Hanoi, the capital of North Vietnam. After he was captured, he spent five and a half years as a prisoner. He later wrote about what happened in a book called Faith of My Fathers. *Most Americans learned of McCain's heroism when he ran for President against George W. Bush during the 2000 Republican primaries.*

I knew I was hit. My plane was spiraling to earth. I didn't think, "Gee, I'm hit. What now?" I reacted the moment I took the hit and saw that my wing was gone. I radioed, "I'm hit," reached up, and pulled the ejection seat handle.

I struck part of the airplane, breaking my left arm, my right arm in three places, and my right knee. I was knocked out by the force of the ejection. I landed in the middle of the lake, in the middle of the city, in the middle of the day.

I came to when I hit the water. Then I blacked out again.

When I came to the second time, I was being **hauled** ashore by a group of about 20 angry Vietnamese. A crowd of several hundred gathered around me. They shouted wildly at me, stripping my clothes off, spitting on me, kicking and striking me…. A woman, who may have been a nurse, began yelling at the crowd. She managed to keep them from further harming me. She then applied bamboo **splints** to my leg and right arm.

I had been shot down a short walk from the prison that the POWs [prisoners of war] had named "the Hanoi Hilton." Its massive steel doors clanked shut behind me….

For four days I was taken back and forth to different rooms. Unable to use my arms, I was fed twice a day by a guard. I vomited after the meals, unable to hold down anything but a little tea. I remember being thirsty all the time. But I could drink only when the guard was present for my twice-daily feedings….

I would remain in **solitary confinement** for over two years.

It's an awful thing, solitary. It crushes your spirit. Having no one else to talk to, you begin to doubt your judgment and your courage. But you adjust to solitary, as you can to almost any hardship. You devise ways to keep your mind off your troubles. And you grasp for any human contact.

—Senator John McCain was released from prison in 1973. In 1986, voters in Arizona elected him to the U.S. Senate.

Heads Up!

Is it a fact that the woman who saved him was a nurse? Or is that McCain's opinion? How can you tell?

The War Hits Home

The Vietnam War was not like other wars. In the past, Americans had seen themselves as being the "good guys." This time people disagreed about who was good or bad. Many people in South Vietnam did not like their own leaders. But in order to fight the Communists, America had taken South Vietnam's side.

Night after night, Americans watched the war **escalate** on television. Civilians had never seen war in such bloody detail. Many were shocked.

By 1971, most Americans were against the war. Hundreds of thousands marched in protest.

Those protests confused our soldiers in Vietnam. Those soldiers were risking their lives. But people at home seemed to have turned against them.

It took the nation a long time to heal from this war. Vietnam veterans deserved the nation's thanks but had to wait a long time to get it.

Finally in 1982, a memorial in Washington, D.C., called "The Wall" was dedicated. It honors the 58,160 American soldiers killed in Vietnam.

Showing the Strain

Paul O'Connell was 17 years old when he enlisted in the Marines. After two months in Vietnam, he was already a hardened veteran.

December 2, 1968

In one of your last letters you wanted to know more about the country. Well, the country is beautiful, except for the barbwire and **bunkers** spread out all over the countryside. The people themselves are filthy and make me sick. You learn not to trust them, and if you can find any reason to shoot them, you do. I've been shot at by too many innocent-looking people to have any mercy. They learn to fire a rifle even before they walk.

—A letter home from Paul O'Connell

Years later, Paul reread that letter and was shocked. Here are his comments on it.

I didn't get to see the letters that I had written to my family for more than 16 years. When my father did give them to me, I found them to be very disturbing, especially this one. Did I really have such an opinion of the Vietnamese while I was there? Hard to admit it, but I probably did. There was so much fear, anger, and frustration in being in Vietnam.

Americans who were protesting the war at home wanted U.S. troops to leave Vietnam. This angered many soldiers who felt betrayed.

November 29, 1970

I'm risking my neck out here in Vietnam because I believe in Freedom. And there are too many people back home NOT worth risking my neck for!

—Captain Frederick Meyer

After months of fighting in jungles, soldiers were exhausted physically and emotionally.

John Houghton wrote this letter to the mother of his good friend Terry J. Perko. Terry was killed in 1967, only five months after arriving in Vietnam. Many soldiers would ask a friend to write to their loved ones, just in case they died in action.

Dear Mrs. Perko,

I'm sorry for not writing sooner. I received your letter when I got out of the hospital in April.

What can I say? I know flowers and letters are fitting, but it's hardly enough....

Some nights I don't sleep. I can't stand being alone at night. The guns don't bother me. I can't hear them anymore. I want to hold my head between my hands and run screaming away from here. I cry too, not much, just when I touch the sore spots.

I'm hollow, Mrs. Perko. I'm a shell, and when I'm scared I rattle. I'm no one to tell you about your son. I can't. I'm sorry.

Johnny Boy

—John "Johnny Boy" Houghton now lives in New Jersey. He works on a tugboat.

Back in America, the war had become very unpopular. Protesters were taking to the streets. There was growing pressure to bring the soldiers home. American troops were starting to leave the country. Some of the soldiers were starting to question what they were doing there. At the time Hector Ramos wrote this letter, the war had been grinding on for years.

August 1969

Things are picking up around here. We're starting to train the Vietnamese to do our jobs. That way they can take over when the time comes for the Air Force to pull out. The local people are not very happy about our leaving. They don't want to lose all the money they are making off the American **GIs.**

We cannot blame them for wanting a way of life that they have never had, and the war is not going to bring any solution. They do not want to fight. They're tired of suffering. They realize this is a war with no gains for the common people.

I've learned only one lesson from this. The United States, as powerful as it may be, cannot play the role of God. It cannot solve all the problems of the world....

Love, Chicky

—Hector Ramos plans electrical systems in New York City. The girlfriend he was writing to in this letter, Yolanda, is now his wife. Chicky was her nickname for him.

Heads Up!

Hector says, "The war is not going to bring any solution." Is that a fact? Or is it Hector's opinion?

Healing Words

Kenneth Peeples, Jr., wrote this letter to his parents two weeks after he was wounded and moved to a hospital in Japan. Kenneth was one of many African Americans who were risking their lives in the war. Meanwhile, back at home the battle for equal rights was still raging.

February 23, 1967
2:30 P.M.

I was just about giving up on mail when I received your letter. It sure did a lot to cheer me up.

To be honest, I'm getting sick and tired of being in a hospital. I'm constantly on my back. I'm not able to walk as yet. It will probably be a few months before I'm even able to try.

This morning they took the cast off, and the doctor changed my dressing. I felt brave enough to peek at my wound for the first time. What I saw didn't make me feel too good. The wound doesn't give me any more pain. But I get a tremendous shock of pain at the sole of my foot and toes. The doctor said it is caused by the damaged nerves. There is nothing they can give me to relieve it. So all I do is just scream day and night. Everyone in the ward knows about it. I yell at the top of my lungs to relieve the pressure. Don't worry, I'll just "scream and bear it" (smile).

I guess I'll try to read a few pages or listen to the radio. My foot is acting up again.

So long for now.

Love,

Kenny

Heads Up!

African-American soldiers risked their lives during the war. But they still struggled for civil rights. Do you think that's fair?

Shortly after Kenneth wrote that letter home, he received this one. It probably cheered him up even more.

February 21, 1967
7:30 P.M.

Hello Son,

How are you feeling today? Hope this letter will find you recovering. Today we received your Purple Heart medal. I looked at it with mixed emotions. Happy, because you are out of Vietnam. Sad, because of the price you had to pay to get away from there. I also realize the thousands of boys who will never return home. Those parents have received the Purple Heart because of their son's death. When I think of these things, I know that I shouldn't feel too bad about your condition.

Let me say here and now that I'm extremely proud of you, son. Not because you were awarded the Heart, but because you did an honorable thing. I know that you were bitterly against going into the service and rejected our reasons for being in Vietnam. I also knew of your feelings about the

U.S. and its treatment of Negroes. Yet, in spite of these conditions, you did everything that was asked of you.

But I do know that you made an honorable decision. It may not matter at all to you, but you are coming home a hero to us. Not a war hero, because you had to fight and get shot, but more so because you made a man's decision and stuck it out. You should feel proud of yourself! You can hold your head high everywhere you go, and you can go anywhere you wish.

You know, I was thinking that for a person who never traveled much, you are really seeing the world. Who would have thought that you would be writing from Japan, and your letters would arrive here in just two days. Hope ours reach you just as fast.

Rest good, and eat hearty. Relax, and don't worry about anything. Will write again soon. Until then, may God continue to bless you.

Love,
Mom & Pop

Nurses and Donut Dollies

An army nurse wrote this poem long after the war. She was looking back on her experiences and found the words for what had been in her heart at the time. Here's how she felt when she had cared for the wounded.

> Hello, David—my name is Dusty.
> I'm your night nurse.
> I will stay with you.
> I will check your **vitals**
>   every 15 minutes.
> I will document
>   **inevitability**
> I will hang more blood
>   and give you something
>   for your pain.

I will stay with you
and I will touch your face.

Yes, of course,
I will write your mother
and tell her you were brave.
I will write your mother
and tell her how much you loved her.
I will write your mother
and tell her to give your bratty kid sister
a big kiss and hug.
What I will not tell her
is that you were wasted.

I will stay with you
and I will hold your hand.
I will stay with you
and watch your life
flow through my fingers
into my soul.
I will stay with you
until you stay with me.
Goodbye, David—my name is Dusty.

I'm the last person
you will see.
I'm the last person
you will touch.
I'm the last person
who will love you.

So long, David—my name is Dusty.
David—who will give me something
for my pain?

**—Dusty served in Vietnam from 1966 to 1968.
She was in the Army Nurse Corps. This poem is
on the Vietnam Memorial in Rochester, New York.**

—Heads Up!—

*What kind of pain do you think Dusty is
feeling at the end of the poem?*

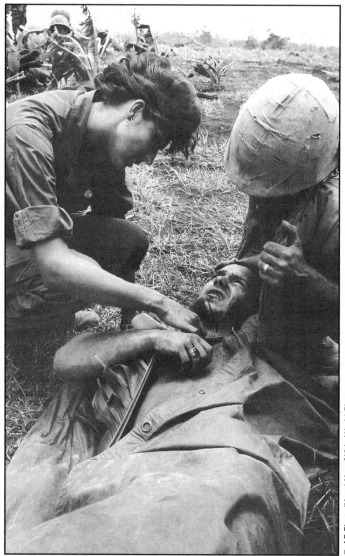

Being an army nurse was risky work. Nine nurses died while serving in Vietnam.

The next letter was written by a "Donut Dolly." These young women worked for the Red Cross. Their job was to provide "a touch of home in a combat zone." Often, they played games with the soldiers, brought them reading material, and wrote letters for them when they were wounded. But mostly they gave them a break from the war.

You asked about Vietnam, so I'll tell you….The work is hard and all the time, but it keeps me on my toes. The men are wonderful. Several times a week we visit the hospitals. This is one of the saddest and yet inspiring jobs for me. Just this past Monday we went to the big Navy hospital…. We saw fellows with their arms and legs blown off. Or their heads are smashed in and pieced together, eyes lost and hearts completely broken. Surprisingly enough, the biggest lift we can give them is a human, female hand and some cheerful words. You know that they feel like hell and then some. But it's an American, a real, live, walking, talking girl! It's amazing to see them perk up. From some it's a feeble attempt to move an arm or even talk.

It's men like that who make it all worthwhile. I would visit and talk with them every day if I could. And yet we're not in the business of giving **sympathy.** Just honest, straight American girl talk. We have to treat them as if nothing were wrong at all, absolutely nothing.

Jeanne

—Jeanne Bokina Christie now works as a teacher in Connecticut.

─Heads Up!─

Look up sympathy *in the glossary. Why do you think the Donut Dollies didn't give the wounded sympathy?*

Good-bye, Vietnam

This letter was famous among soldiers during the war. No one is sure who wrote it. But it seemed to express the feelings of many. The tone of the letter is humorous but the humor is a little dark. The soldiers had been through a lot. In order to survive they had to learn to laugh instead of cry. That's part of what this letter tries to explain.

Dear Civilians, Friends, Draft Dodgers, etc.:

In the very near future, this soldier will once more be in your midst. In your joy at welcoming him back, you might make some allowances for the past twelve months. In other words, he should be handled with care. Don't be alarmed if he is infected with all forms of rare tropical diseases....

Show no alarm if he insists on carrying a weapon to the dinner table. He may look around for his steel pot [helmet] when offered a chair. He might wake you up in the middle of the night for guard duty. Keep cool when he pours gravy on his dessert at dinner. Pretend not to notice if he acts dazed or eats with his fingers instead of silverware. He may prefer **C-rations** to steak. Be tolerant when he takes his blanket and sheet off the bed and goes to sleep on the floor.

Say nothing about powdered eggs, dried potatoes, fried rice, fresh milk, or ice cream. Also, if it should start raining, pay no attention to him. He will pull off his clothes, grab a bar of soap and a towel, and run outdoors for a shower. Pretend not to notice if he uses his hat as an ashtray.

Above all, keep in mind that beneath that rough outside there is a heart of gold. It is the only thing of value he has left. Treat him with kindness and tolerance. You will be able to bring back the happy-go-lucky guy you once knew and loved.

Last, but not least, send no more mail

to Vietnam. Fill the icebox with beer, get his clothes out of mothballs, fill the car with gas... BECAUSE THE KID IS COMING HOME!!!!!

Love, Dave

Different versions of this letter were passed around by soldiers in Vietnam.

Heads Up!

Why do you think soldiers liked this letter so much?

Larry Jackson flew Army helicopters in Vietnam. This is a letter to his mother.

September 11, 1969

… Coming home pretty soon. Going to quit flying soon, too much for me now. I have flown 1,500 hours now, and in those hours I could tell you a lifetime story. I have been put in for a medal again, but this time I have seen far beyond of whatever you will see. That is why I'm going to quit flying. I dream of Valerie's hand touching mine telling me to come home; but I wake up, and it's some sergeant telling me I have to fly. Today I am 21, far away but coming home older.

Love,

Larry

—Larry Jackson was killed less than 24 hours after he wrote this letter.

Because the Vietnam War had become so unpopular, not all soldiers were welcomed home with open arms.

Welcome Home

Ted McCormick's parents met him when he arrived at the airport in Detroit, Michigan. Like it was for many soldiers, his homecoming was bittersweet.

I was standing by the luggage counter waiting for my duffle bag to come down the chute. My parents in their excitement had failed to see me. I stood and watched them for a minute, thinking about the many times I had thought about them, lying in the jungle and staring at the stars, wondering what they were doing at that particular moment in time and if I would ever see them again....

I stepped forward, and they saw me. We embraced and greeted each other. My father's words were profound. He shook my hand, placed his left hand on my shoulder, and said, "You can put all of this behind you now, son. It's all over. Glad to have you back. We missed you."

Tears swelled up in my eyes. He had no idea. I had never explained to my family what I was really involved in, trying to keep the ugly side of warfare from them. They knew that I was in an **infantry** unit. But in my letters, I was vague about my role in this war.

Here I was standing in a daze. After fighting in the jungles of Viet Nam and Laos for a year, living like an animal, I was in shock in my own country. I had been permanently changed by my experiences, and I had been afraid to come home.

—After leaving the Army, Ted McCormick got a job with an automaker in Detroit.

Heads Up!

Why do you think that Ted wanted to keep the "ugly side of warfare" from his family?

Michael Murphy spent two years on the USS *Coral Sea, an aircraft carrier.*

I have been in the Navy for two years and this is the end of my second tour to Vietnam. My wife Jeanne will be in San Francisco to greet me upon my arrival. My mother, father, aunt and uncle will be there as well. They saw me off before the first tour so it is nice that they will be here when I come home.

I stay on the flight deck until we dock. It's a time to think and reflect on the times that have passed during the past two years. Times containing laughter and fun, but not overshadowing the episodes of death and pain....

I can see the [San Francisco Golden Gate Bridge] clearer now, as well as the surrounding land. You just don't know how good it feels to see America.

The USS *Coral Sea* had been adopted by the City of San Francisco two years before. Last year the city put on a nice homecoming for us. I hope they do the same this time; it really means a lot to us....

The bridge is getting closer now. I can see people waving to us. Last year they had a sign that said "Welcome Home," and they dropped flowers from the bridge....

We are passing under the bridge now. The people are shouting [dirty words] and are dumping garbage on us. A sign unfolds. It says "MURDERERS." A terrible [emptiness] fills my heart as if someone just kicked me in the chest. My country asked me to go. I went. I did what was expected of me as an American. I did not run away from my duty. I fought for what I believed in, freedom. Was I wrong?

—Michael Murphy served off Vietnam's shores from 1967 to 1969.

Heads Up!

The protesters called the sailors murderers. Was it a fact that they were murderers? Or was it an opinion?

Mike Kelly was badly wounded in Vietnam. He spent a year in a hospital in San Francisco.

When I was released from [the hospital], there seemed to be more enemies here than there had been in Vietnam.... Much later that night the bus delivered me and my duffle bag to downtown Sacramento, but still some ten miles short of home. It was much too early in the morning to wake up the family. I stood alone on that deserted street pondering the next step when a cab drove by. I waved him down.

He looked me over carefully before saying a word. "You just back from the war?" he asked. I told him that, in a way, yes, that was true.

I braced for what might follow, that he might deliver a lecture and boot me out. But all he said was, "Where you headed?" and I told him the address.

"Okay, this ride's on me."

Not another word was spoken until he pulled to a stop in front of my folk's house and offered me his hand. "Thanks," he said. "Good luck, kid." And he was gone.

It took me a while before I found the [self-control] to quietly let myself in and start again the life I'd left behind. I sat there in the living room, all alone except for the family's beloved and equally delighted Irish setter. I hugged and stroked him while he licked my face clean of the tears that had found their way down my cheek. They were tears coming not from the joy of being home, but from the memory of the cabbie's simple offering of welcome and thanks. I would never forget that morning or the kindness of that wonderful man.

**—Mike Kelly served in
Vietnam in 1969 and 1970.**

Heads Up!

Why was Mike Kelly surprised by what the cab driver did?

10

Making Peace

Like many veterans, Nancy Smoyer returned to Vietnam to make peace with her memories.

In April 1993, I went back to Vietnam for a month with [other veterans]. Our group was small—three combat veterans and myself, a Red Cross Donut Dolly.

We spent two weeks fixing up a clinic at Cu Chi. Then there were two weeks traveling north to Hanoi. We worked and traveled with former Viet Cong and NVA [North Vietnamese Army] soldiers. This added something unexpected but very welcome to the experience, because I was stationed at Cu Chi. I met a fellow worker, and learned that he had been at Cu Chi during the entire war. Then I realized that this man was

This Vietnam veteran is paying his respects at a Vietnamese graveyard.

lobbing **mortars** and rockets at me during [the Tet Offensive in 1968]. It was a strange feeling. But during the two weeks we worked together on the clinic, we formed a special bond. He gave me his gold star pin. I gave him a pin from the tenth anniversary of the Wall. We joked and teased and spoke of friendship and peace. His face became the face that made the enemy human for me.

The most important thing that happened was a change I found myself going through during my first week there. It took me by surprise. My main reason for going back was to get over the feelings of anger I've carried for the Vietnamese for 25 years. Although I knew that my feelings did not make sense, I also knew that I would not get over them until I went back. The anger I have felt has been toward the Vietnamese people and the Vietnamese government. And I was angry with the American people and the American government. Those feelings of anger have spilled over to many parts of my life. And then there was the sadness. It was hitting me full force again right then and there.

As I understood this, I knew that I had already lost my anger toward the Vietnamese people. I worked with the Vietnamese veterans. I went into their homes. I met their families. I saw pictures in every home we visited of family members who had died in the war. I saw the huge graveyards and memorials to the war dead. I heard about the 300,000 Vietnamese who are still missing. And after this, I could not continue carrying my angry feelings. I gained an understanding that I had not allowed myself to feel before. I had done what I came back to Vietnam to do.

Now I have two Vietnams. I have the one in my memory, and the Vietnamese Vietnam. It had been "my" country for a while—my GI Vietnam. And yet it was theirs, and should have been, all along.

—Nancy Smoyer was a Red Cross Recreation Worker, or Donut Dolly.

Glossary

bunker *(noun)* an underground shelter (p. 30)

C-ration *(noun)* canned food for soldiers (p. 47)

civilian *(noun)* anyone who is not a member of the armed forces (p. 20)

Communism *(noun)* the belief that the people should own equal portions of a nation's land and its wealth (p. 12)

conflict *(noun)* a war or period of fighting (p. 12)

escalate *(verb)* to increase in amount or intensity (p. 29)

GI *(noun)* an American soldier. GI is short for Government Issue. (p. 34)

guerrilla warfare *(noun)* fighting by small groups who are not part of a regular army (p. 12)

haul *(verb)* to pull or drag (p. 26)

inevitability *(noun)* events that can't be changed or avoided (p. 40)

infantry *(noun)* soldiers that fight on foot (p. 52)

influence *(verb)* to have an effect on something or someone (p. 12)

leech *(noun)* a blood-sucking worm (p. 13)

mortar *(noun)* a short cannon that shoots shells or rockets (p. 59)

North Vietnam *(noun)* the part of Vietnam controlled by Communists (p. 12)

platoon *(noun)* a group of soldiers under one command (p. 18)

solitary confinement *(noun)* keeping a prisoner in a cell apart from all others (p. 27)

South Vietnam *(noun)* the part of Vietnam the U. S. tried to protect from the Communists (p. 12)

splint *(noun)* a support for an injured limb (p. 27)

sympathy *(noun)* pity or sorrow for another's pain (p. 45)

veteran *(noun)* someone who has served in the armed forces, especially during a war (p. 9)

Viet Cong *(noun)* also called VC; Communist soldiers from South Vietnam who fought on the side of North Vietnam (p. 12)

vitals *(noun)* vital signs: breathing, pulse, and other signs of life (p. 40)

Index

Acknowledgments

Grateful acknowledgment is made to the following sources for permission to reprint from previously published material. The publisher has made diligent efforts to trace the ownership of all copyrighted material in this volume and believes that all necessary permissions have been secured. If any errors or omissions have inadvertently been made, proper corrections will gladly be made in future editions.

p. 9: Richard Ford letter from BLOODS: AN ORAL HISTORY OF THE VIETNAM WAR BY BLACK VETERANS by Wallace Terry. Copyright © 1984 by Wallace Terry. Reprinted by permission of Random House, Inc.

p. 10: Thomas Bird letter from EVERYTHING WE HAD: AN ORAL HISTORY OF THE VIETNAM WAR BY THIRTY-THREE AMERICAN SOLDIERS WHO FOUGHT IT by Al Santoli and Albert Santoli. Copyright © 1981 by Albert Santoli and Vietnam Veterans of America. Reprinted by permission of Random House, Inc.

p. 11: Paul O'Connell letter from *The Vietnam Veterans Home Page* web site. Copyright © 1996 by Paul E. O'Connell. Reprinted by permission of the author.

p. 13–14: Salvador Gonzalez letter from DEAR AMERICA: LETTERS HOME FROM VIETNAM, edited by Bernard Edelman. Copyright © 1985 by The New York Vietnam Veterans Memorial Commission. Published by W. W. Norton & Company, Inc. Reprinted by permission of Bernard Edelman.

p. 15–17: Henry Romero letter from DEAR AMERICA: LETTERS HOME FROM VIETNAM, edited by Bernard Edelman. Copyright © 1985 by The New York Vietnam Veterans Memorial Commission. Published by W. W. Norton & Company, Inc. Reprinted by permission of Bernard Edelman.

p. 18–19: From "An Tan" by Mike Bailey from *Mike Company, Third Battalion, First Marines* web site. Copyright © 1999 by Mike Bailey. Reprinted by permission of the author.

p. 20–22: George Williams letter from DEAR AMERICA: LETTERS HOME FROM VIETNAM, edited by Bernard Edelman. Copyright © 1985 by The New York Vietnam Veterans Memorial Commission. Published by W. W. Norton & Company, Inc. Reprinted by permission of Bernard Edelman.

p. 23–24: Kenneth Peeples letter from DEAR AMERICA: LETTERS HOME FROM VIETNAM, edited by Bernard Edelman. Copyright © 1985 by The New York Vietnam Veterans Memorial Commission. Published by W. W. Norton & Company, Inc. Reprinted by permission of Bernard Edelman.

p. 26–28: Adapted from FAITH OF MY FATHERS by John McCain and Mark Salter. Copyright © 1999 by John McCain and Mark Salter. Reprinted by permission of Random House, Inc.

p. 30–31: Paul O'Connell letter and commentary from *The Vietnam Veterans Home Page* web site. Copyright © 1996 by Paul E. O'Connell. Reprinted by permission of the author.

p. 31: Frederick Meyer letter from *War Letters: Rochester Writes Home* web site. All rights reserved.

p. 33: John Houghton letter from DEAR AMERICA: LETTERS HOME FROM VIETNAM, edited by Bernard Edelman. Copyright © 1985 by The New York Vietnam Veterans Memorial Commission. Published by W. W. Norton & Company, Inc. Reprinted by permission of Bernard Edelman.

p. 34–35: Hector Ramos letter from DEAR AMERICA: LETTERS HOME FROM VIETNAM, edited by Bernard Edelman. Copyright © 1985 by The New York Vietnam Veterans Memorial Commission. Published by W. W. Norton & Company, Inc. Reprinted by permission of Bernard Edelman.

p. 36–39: Kenneth Peeples letter and letter from parents from DEAR AMERICA: LETTERS HOME FROM VIETNAM, edited by Bernard Edelman. Copyright © 1985 by The New York Vietnam Veterans Memorial Commission. Published by W. W. Norton & Company, Inc. Reprinted by permission of Bernard Edelman.

p. 40–42: "Hello David" from SHRAPNEL IN THE HEART by Laura Palmer. Copyright © 1987 by Laura Palmer. Reprinted by permission of Random House, Inc.

p. 44–45: Jeanne Bokina Christie letter from DEAR AMERICA: LETTERS HOME FROM VIETNAM, edited by Bernard Edelman. Copyright © 1985 by The New York Vietnam Veterans Memorial Commission. Published by W. W. Norton & Company, Inc. Reprinted by permission of Bernard Edelman.

p. 46–48: David Bowman letter from DEAR AMERICA: LETTERS HOME FROM VIETNAM, edited by Bernard Edelman. Copyright © 1985 by The New York Vietnam Veterans Memorial Commission. Published by W. W. Norton & Company, Inc. Reprinted by permission of Bernard Edelman.

p. 49: Larry Jackson letter from *The Vietnam Veterans Home Page* web site. Copyright © by Mark Jackson. All rights reserved.

p. 51–52: From "Hill 882" by Ted McCormick from *Nam Magazine*, May 2002. Copyright © 1997 by Ted McCormick. All rights reserved.

p. 53–54: From "Welcome Home" by Michael Murphy from *The Vietnam Veterans Home Page* web site. Copyright © 1999 by Michael L. Murphy. Reprinted by permission of the author.

p. 55–56: From "Coming Home" by Mike Kelley from *The Vietnam Veterans Home Page* web site. Copyright © 1998 by Mike Kelley. Reprinted by permission of the author.

p. 57–60: From "Making Peace" by Nancy Smoyer from *The Vietnam Veterans Home Page* web site. Copyright © 1994 by Nancy Smoyer. Reprinted by permission of the author.